*"I hear within me
as from a spring of living water
the murmur:*

COME TO THE FATHER.*"*

Saint Ignatius of Antioch

COME TO THE Father

Pupil's Text *(revised 1972)*
THE CANADIAN CATECHISM

PAULIST PRESS
NEW YORK, N.Y. / RAMSEY, N.J

CCCB
Ottawa, Canada

Cat. No. 1-100

The Canadian Catechism, in this English revised edition, is the result of collaboration between the Office de Catéchèse du Québec, Montréal, Québec, The National Office of Religious Education, Ottawa, and the Office National d'Education Chrétienne, Ottawa, Canada.

APPROVED:
by the Canadian Bishops
Wilfrid E. Doyle, J.C.D., D.D., Président,
Office of Religious Education, English Sector,
Canadian Catholic Conference, August 13, 1971
and
Gérard-Marie Coderre, D.D., Président,
Office of Religious Education, French Sector,
Canadian Catholic Conference, August 30, 1971

EDITORIAL TEAM:
FRENCH EDITION:
Jean-Paul Bérubé, team leader
Marcel Caron, Françoise Darcy, Martin Jeffery,
Alberte Julien, Renée-Dubeau Legentil,
Suzanne Lévesque, Réginald Marsolais,
Margaret Ordway, André Turmel, Bruno Vezeau.

ENGLISH EDITION:
May O'Hanlon, team leader
Lawrence DeMong, Martin Jeffery.
With the collaboration of the
Catechetical Institute of Quebec,
the team for pastoral in the elementary
division of the Catholic Schools of Montreal
and the diocesan offices of French
and English Canada.

DESIGN AND GRAPHICS:
Kenneth Riopelle

Published by
Paulist Press
1865 Broadway
New York, N.Y. 10023
and by
Canadian Conference of
Catholic Bishops
90 Parent Ave.
Ottawa, Canada K1N7B1

COPYRIGHT:
© 1972 by Office de Catéchèse du Québec,
Montréal, Canada.

ACKNOWLEDGMENT:
Excerpts from the Jerusalem Bible, Copyright©
1966 by Darton, Longman & Todd, Ltd. and
Doubleday & Company, Inc. Reprinted by
permission of the publisher.

PRINTED AND BOUND
In the United States of America

PHOTOS:
Paul Bilodeau: page 3
Pierre Gaudard: pages 10-12 A-18-30 C-D-55-
57-75 C
John Kelly: page 11
Fred Lyon from Rapho Guillumette: pages 12-13
Kiraly: page 14-75B
P. Peyskens: pages 15-37-56-70-76
Sicot: pages 19-20-67
Ed. Lettau: pages 27-33-36-74
N.F.B.: pages 30 B-54-64
Victor Charbonneau: page 34
B.P. Audio Visual: page 44
Bruce Roberts from Rapho Guillumette: page 58
Peter Mlller from Rapho Guillumette: page 61
Jerry Cranham from Rapho Guillumette: page 65
Ellefsen: page 66

ILLUSTRATIONS:
by Jeanne Courtemanche-Auclair

ISBN 0 88760 021 2

TO PARENTS

This is the new edition of Book 1 of the Canadian Catechism series.

Our aim is the same as in the first edition: to help the child develop, within his own experience, a relationship with the Father, Son, and Holy Spirit.

Some changes have been made in response to the wishes of parents, priests, and teachers. They are intended to help adapt the catechesis to the abilities of the child.

The content of the lessons has been shortened and simplified.

There are many new illustrations.

The "parent pages" which used to be in the child's book are now in a separate book.

This book represents another effort on the part of the clergy and laity working together to improve your child's religious education.

May it help you as a parent to carry out your responsibility of leading your child to the Father, through the Son, in the Holy Spirit.

CONTENTS

1
I DISCOVER MYSELF

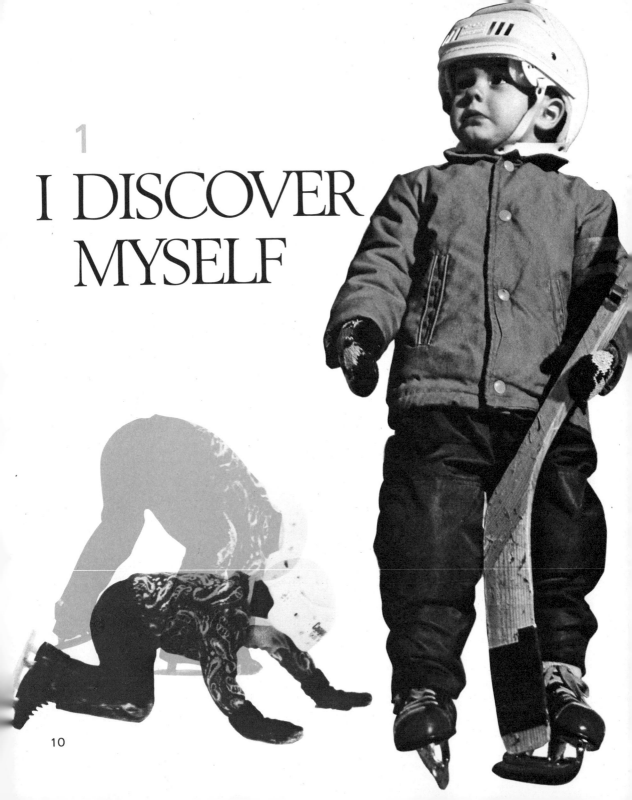

2

I MAKE NEW FRIENDS

I learn my friends' names.
It's fun to work and play together.

3
GOD OUR FATHER GIVES ME LIFE

It's great to be alive.
I can have so much fun.

4 I ADMIRE ALL THAT

IS BEAUTIFUL

17

Do you like to see the sunshine?
Do you like to hear the running water?

Do you like to play with pets
and look at birds and animals?

When you admire these things,
you can say to God our Father:

Lord, how great and wonderful you are.

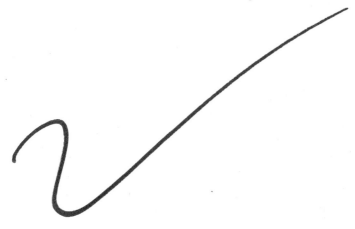

5

I AM FILLED WITH AT GOD OUR FATHER

Sun and moon, bless the Lord.
Day and night, bless the Lord.
All you animals, bless the Lord.
Praise him, exalt him forever.

(Song 5)

WONDER

6

I PRAISE GOD OUR FATHER

I tell God our Father
  he is very great, he is very good.
  He gives me all that is beautiful.
  ALLELUIA!

All the earth proclaim the Lord,
Sing your praise to God.

(Song 6)

7 JESUS TELLS US ABOUT

Jesus says to us:

"All that I have heard from my Father
I have made known to you."

(Adapted from John 15,15)

We can answer:

Lord, open my heart to your words.

We can sing:

All you nations,
sing out your joy to the Lord.
ALLELUIA, ALLELUIA.

(Song 14)

GOD OUR FATHER

8 GOD IS OUR FATHER

Jesus tells us:

"God my Father is your Father too."

With Jesus we can say to God our Father:

Our Father who art in heaven,
hallowed be thy name.
Thy kingdom come.
Thy will be done on earth
as it is in heaven.

9

GOD OUR FATHER LOOKS AT ME WITH LOVE

We listen to the Word of God:
> "I love you with an everlasting love.
> I will always love you."

(Adapted from Isaiah 54, 8 and 10)

10
GOD OUR FATHER KNOWS ME BY MY NAME

God our Father says to each one of us:

"I have called you by your name. You are mine."

(Adapted from Isaiah 43,1)

We can answer:

Yes, Lord, I am all yours.

MARK DENISE ELISA RAYMO
ALEXANDER SE ROBERT
THEE JOSEPH PAUL ANDREW CAT
LAWRENCE ED PAUL VERONICA
KEN DEBORAH JENNIFER
JAMES JONALGIA GEORG
JOHN DONALD NANCY
CAROL PETER THOMAS SELINA
DOROTHY

11
GOD OUR FATHER
JOY OF THINKING

God wanted man to be like him.
He gave him a heart to think with.

(Adapted from Sirach 17, 1.5)

We can answer:
<u>O God our Father,</u>
you want us to live.
You give us the joy of thinking.
We thank you.

GIVES ME THE

12

GOD OUR FATHER GIVES ME THE JOY WORKING

It's good to be able to work!

Those who work make the world more beautiful.
They resemble God our Father
who makes all things beautiful.
What we do, we do for you, Lord.
We offer ourselves to you.

OF

13

GOD OUR FATHER GIVES ME THE JOY OF LOVING

We know a new name for God.

GOD IS LOVE.

Because God is love, he gives us the joy of loving.

We can sing:

God is love and he who abides in love
abides in God and God in him.

(Song 10)

14
WE GREET THE VIRGIN MARY

Mary said to God:

"I am the handmaid of the Lord;
let what you have said be done to me."

(Luke 1,38)

With all Christians we greet the Virgin Mary:

Hail Mary, full of grace,
the Lord is with thee.
Blessed art thou among women,
and blessed is the fruit of thy womb, Jesus.

Song:

Hail Mary, our Mother,
you are filled with God's love.
Yes, Lord; yes, I come.
I am ready to do all you ask.

(Song 11)

15
WE CELEBRATE CHRISTMAS

We listen to God's Word:

"Yes, God loved the world so much that he gave his only Son."

(John 3,16)

We can say:

Lord Jesus, you are the Father's Son.
You have come to us.
We adore you and we believe in you.

JESUS CAME FOR ALL THE PEOPLES OF

Jesus came for us:

> for our parents and our friends,
> for the rich and the poor,
> for the great and the small.
> He came for all the peoples of the earth.

THE EARTH

JESUS GROWS UP IN

Jesus lived like us:

he was small;
he grew up;
he learned to work;
he learned to love.

We can sing:

Praise Christ, the Son of the living God.
Praise Christ, the Word of the living God.
Praise Christ, the Light of the living God, alleluia.

(Song 15)

NAZARETH

18
JESUS SAYS TO US: HAVE TRUST

Jesus said to the crowds:

"Look at the birds in the sky.
Your heavenly Father feeds them.
And look at the flowers in the fields.
They are very beautiful.
It is your heavenly Father who wants them to be like this
But you, you are worth more than the birds,
more than the flowers. The Father loves you;
put your trust in him."

(Adapted from Matthew 6,25-34 and John 16,27)

We can say:

God our Father,
I put my trust in you.

19

JESUS IS GOOD LIKE GOD HIS FATHER

Jesus says:

"Let the little children come to me;
do not stop them;
for God's house is for them."

(Adapted from Mark 10, 14)

We can say to Jesus:

Lord Jesus,
you are good,
you love us
as God our Father does.
We trust you.

49

20
JESUS INTRODUCES HOLY SPIRIT

The Lord Jesus says to us:
"I am not alone,
because the Father is with me."
(Adapted from John 16,32)

"The spirit of the Lord has been given to me."
(Luke 4,18)

Often Jesus went alone to a mountain
to pray to God his Father.
The Holy Spirit was with him,
uniting him to the Father.

We can say:
Glory be to the Father, and to the Son, and
to the Holy Spirit, as it was in the beginning is
now and ever shall be, world without end. Amen.

US TO THE

21
THE HOLY SPIRIT IS ALWAYS WITH US

We listen to God's Word:

"Alone we do not know how to pray as we ought to.
The Holy Spirit teaches us to pray to the Father."

(Adapted from Romans 8,26)

We can say:

Thank you, God our Father,
for your Holy Spirit.

22
MY MOMENTS OF HAPPINESS

Everybody wants to be happy.
   I do too!

I am happy when people are kind to me,
   when people play with me.

I am happy also
   when I am kind to others,
   when I make them happy.

23

I DISCOVER HOW I CAN SHARE HAPPINESS

Jesus says to us:

"You are my friends when you love one another."

(Adapted from John 13,35)

We can ask the Lord Jesus:

Lord Jesus, teach us
to please God our Father
by loving each other.

24
SHARING HAPPINESS LIKE JESUS

Jesus is good to everyone.
He pleases God his Father.
Often in his heart he says:
> "Here I am, Father, I have come to do your will."

(Hebrews 10,7)

We can say:
> We give you thanks, Father,
> through your Son Jesus
> with the Spirit of love. Amen.

61

25 JESUS INVITES

Jesus says to Zacchaeus:

"Zacchaeus, come down quickly.
Today, I want to eat with you."

(Luke 19,5)

We are able to say to Jesus:

Like Zacchaeus, I want to be your friend.
Give me your Spirit.
Help me to become better.

JS TO BE BETTER

26
JESUS TEACHES US HOW TO FORGIVE

Often it is hard to love,
to share and above all to forgive.
But the Holy Spirit has been given to us
to help us love, even when it is hard.

With the Spirit of Jesus we can say to God our Father:

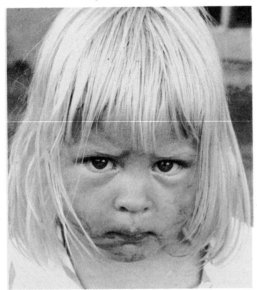

Forgive us our trespasses
as we forgive those
who trespass against us.

27

WE RECALL
JESUS' GREAT LOVE

We listen to God's Word:

"God loved the world so much that he
gave his only Son
so that all men would be saved
through him."

(Adapted from John 3, 16-17)

We can say to Jesus:

Lord Jesus, you have always loved us;
you loved us, even when it was hard.
You gave your life to save us.
Thank you, Lord Jesus.

28
THE LORD JESUS IS RISEN

On Easter day the Lord Jesus
rose, as he said.
> ALLELUIA.

We can say:
Christ has died.
Christ is risen.
Christ will come again.

29

ONE DAY WE SHALL RISE LIKE JESUS

We listen to the Word of God:

"God who raised up his Son Jesus
will by his power raise us too."

(Adapted from 1 Corinthians 6,14)

We can say:

God our Father, we trust in your Word.
We believe that you will raise us up
by the power of the Holy Spirit,
just as you raised your Son Jesus.
We thank you, Father. Amen.

30
CHRISTIANS CELEBRATE

On Sunday, Christians gather together.
They celebrate the resurrection
of the Lord Jesus.

They remember Jesus' Word:

> "Where two or three
> meet in my name,
> I shall be there with them."

(Matthew 18,20)

We can say:

> This is the day the Lord made.
> It is a day of joy. Alleluia.

THE LORD JESUS

31

AT THE EUCHARIST WE PRAISE AND THANK THE FATHER WITH JESUS

Always and everywhere
but especially at the Eucharist,
we can praise and bless God our Father
and thank him for all his goodness.

He sent us his Son Jesus.
He raised him from the dead.
He gives us the Holy Spirit
who puts love in our hearts.

32

THE CHURCH IS THE GOD'S CHILDREN

When a <u>baby</u> is baptized, we celebrate and welcome him into the Church, the family of God's children.

See how much the Father loves us.
We are God's <u>children</u>. (Adapted from 1 John 3,1)

With Jesus we can say:

I praise and thank you, Father,
Lord of heaven and of earth,
for having made known your secrets
to little ones.

(Adapted from Luke 10,21)

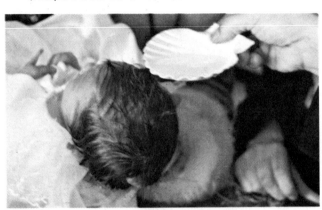

FAMILY OF